LANDSCAPE INTO SOUND

LANDSCAPE INTO SOUND

David Matthews

The Claridge Press
St Albans

First published in Great Britain 1992

by The Claridge Press
27 Windridge Close
St Albans
Herts
AL3 4JP

Copyright   ©   David Matthews

Published in association with the Peter Fuller Memorial Foundation

Printed by
Short Run Press
Exeter, Devon

ISBN 1-870626-28-1

1.   Art and Music

PREFACE AND ACKNOWLEDGEMENTS

Landscape into Sound is a revised and slightly expanded version of
the first Peter Fuller Lecture given at the Tate Gallery in Liverpool
and London in June and July 1991. I was aware while writing the
lecture that the subject was far bigger than I could hope to encom-
pass within the time allotted, so that, inevitably, there are huge areas
left undiscussed. The recorded music examples which were an
integral part of the lecture obviously could not be provided here, but
I have included most of them in short score form for those who can
read music.

I knew Peter Fuller for only a brief period before his tragic death.
Music was not something that he ever wrote about, although certain
pieces of music meant a great deal to him, most of them English, and
above all the music of Elgar. A month or so before he died, Peter
asked me to send him some tapes of contemporary music, and he had
hoped that I might be able to help him fill in the gaps in his
knowledge about what composers today were up to. I was very
touched to discover that the last music Peter heard was one of my
own pieces. Given his restlessly exploring mind, I am sure it would
only have been a matter of time before he drew music into a still
more comprehensive view of art. So in writing about some of the
connections I have sensed between music and painting, I feel I am
venturing into an area that Peter himself might, in a quite different
way and with his own special authority, have been dealing with by
now.

For permission to print copyright music examples, I am grateful
to the following publishers: Faber Music Limited (David Matthews,
Concertino), Universal Edition (London) Limited (Webern, String
Quartet, op. 28), Edition Peters, London (Schoenberg, Five Pieces

for Orchestra, op. 16), Boosey and Hawkes Limited (Britten, *Peter Grimes*) and Oxford University Press (Vaughan Williams, Symphony no. 5). I am also most grateful to the various galleries and institutions in which the paintings illustrated are housed for their permission to reproduce them. Details of its location will be found with each illustration.

I must also acknowledge here my debt to Edward Lockspeiser's book *Music and Painting*, the only study I know to have examined the relationship in depth, and which gave me a starting point for my lecture; also to Christopher Palmer's perceptive essay on *Peter Grimes* in *The Britten Companion* (Faber, 1984). I should also like to thank Robin Leanse and Roger Scruton for valuable suggestions. I am grateful to Stephanie McDonald and the trustees of the Peter Fuller Memorial Foundation for inviting me to give the lecture in the first place, and for generously assisting its publication.

David Matthews, May, 1992

LANDSCAPE INTO SOUND

While most people have practised painting and writing at least on the simplest level, relatively few ever write music and perhaps for that reason music is often thought of as a mysterious outsider in relation to the other arts. Music and painting might seem at first to be two entirely separate non-verbal languages. Each has its own techniques; each inhabits its own dimension and appeals to its own sense: music inhabits time, painting space; you hear one, you see the other. It isn't quite as simple as that: the dimension of time must also enter into our appreciation of a painting, if we are thoroughly to explore its meaning; while music at its greatest approaches the stillness that is at the heart of a great painting. And there are other, more mundane points of contact between music and painting, which have not often been discussed. I have chosen to focus on a few areas that have particularly interested me, as a composer who has always loved painting and often been much moved by what I have seen, to the extent that on two occasions the experience of seeing a painting has led me to compose music about it.

Music sometimes appears to be about nothing but itself: that is to say, the composer usually begins from a simple melodic or harmonic idea, and from that first idea others may come, and he fashions them with his acquired skills into a piece, with the same care for formal balance that the painter must possess, and the sense of timing that the good composer shares with the good playwright. But where do musical ideas come from in the first place? Anything that happens in his life may move the composer to express himself in music. A painting may be highly suggestive of music, as I shall try to show. I shall also show how some of the techniques of music may be compared to those of painting, and how landscape has sometimes been and continues to be a common source of inspiration for composers and painters. This is a composer's point of view, and I can't speak for those many painters whom I know to have found inspiration in music. That complementary approach would be an essay in itself.

***

Music and painting come together most literally in those many depictions of musicians playing instruments or singing, that are present from the very beginning of visual art: from the harpists in Assyrian bas-reliefs, Greek vase paintings of *kithara* and *aulos* players, through Fra Angelico's angel choirs and Vermeer's virginalists, their music frozen into silence, down to Chagall's folk-violinists and Picasso's guitarists.

We look at these paintings and may try to imagine what music the musicians are playing. A few years ago I looked at Titian's *Flaying of Marsyas* and the eventual result was a piece of my own. I had seen this tremendous late painting in the Royal Academy's Venice exhibition; three years later I happened to be in Czechoslovakia and was able to go to Kroměříž where the painting has its home, in the palace of the archbishops of Olomouc. I had been asked to compose a piece for oboe and string quartet, but at that time I had no idea what I was going to do. When I saw the painting again, it struck me with particular force that what chiefly redeems the horrifying subject-matter is the figure of the musician, who may or may not be Apollo, playing what in fact is a *lira da braccio*, but which I heard there and then as violin music, broad and sustained, calming the violence of the flaying. I realised I had a solution for my piece, which could enact the competition between Apollo and Marsyas, Apollo being represented by the first violin and Marsyas, who played the *aulos*, which is usually translated as flute but is actually a reed instrument, by the oboe. In the passage that depicts the flaying (Ex.1 shows its beginning), Apollo's violin music is in direct conflict with the oboe's cries of pain. Marsyas dies, as the oboe stutters into silence.

But he returns; for in one version of the myth, his blood became a river, on the banks of which men made oboes: so his music continues. In my piece (which was eventually called simply *Concertino* as I decided not to stress the programmatic element) Marsyas' redemption occurs when the oboe takes over Apollo's music for himself.

Ex.1

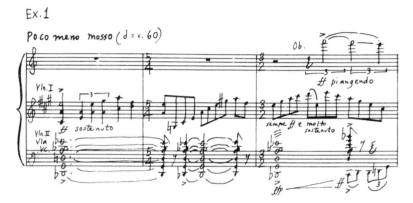

I want to look at another painting by Titian, *Venus and the Organ Player*. There are several versions of this painting. In the most authentic one, which is in Berlin, the background is a mountain landscape, and the main mountain distantly mirrors the organ pipes, which are also suggested, upside down, by the hanging fold of the drapery on the right. In another version, in the Prado, the background of trees and the path in front of the trees on the left cunningly mirror the organ pipes and the keyboard. In both versions it is not what the organist may be playing that immediately interests me so much as what the background landscape suggests, and the Prado painting is especially suggestive: the figure on the path turning to look at the statue as the organ player turns to look at Venus, and the two lines of trees drawing the spectator out of the picture towards the infinity of the sunlit horizon. If we now come back to the organist, perhaps after all what he is playing is what the background landscape seems so eloquently to be expressing. So that now it might be

Titian: *The Flaying of Marsyas*

Archbishop's Palace, Kroměříž

Titian: *Venus and the Organ Player*

Museo Nacional del Prado, Madrid

possible to write his piece, and for it to become the theme of an extended fantasy that developed away from it, just as the painting moves us forward and away into its own fantasy. At any rate that's one way in which this painting might be translated into music.

Schopenhauer said that "the deep relation which music has to the true nature of all things...explains the fact that suitable music played to any scene, action, event, or surrounding seems to disclose to us its most secret meaning, and appears to us as the most accurate and distinct commentary on it." Accompanying paintings with music has become a cliché of television arts programmes, but in most cases the chosen music matches the painting only in the most general sense. For an example of true affinity between a painting and a piece of music, I would suggest that a landscape by Friedrich — for instance his *Bohemian Landscape* of 1810 -- might be accompanied by the music of Bruckner. I have no idea whether Bruckner was at all interested in painting; I rather doubt it. But his religious apprehension of nature -- for I am sure this is nature music in its deepest sense -- is uncannily similar to Friedrich's, and the profound stillness of Friedrich's landscapes, especially those with distant mountains, finds its exact musical equivalent in those passages in Bruckner such as the beginning of the development in the first movement of the Eighth Symphony (Ex.2), where the music opens out into vast spaces and there is a feeling of mysterious grandeur.

Ex. 2

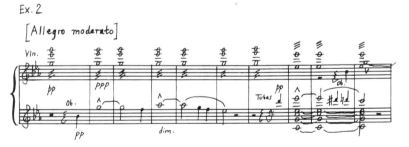

In another example of close correspondence of feeling, composer and painter are historically quite far apart. I have always thought that Berlioz's 'Royal Hunt and Storm' from *The Trojans* (Ex. 3) captures the spirit of Claude -- most particularly his very last painting, in the Ashmolean, which is another hunt involving Aeneas' son Ascanius.

In such music, Berlioz's Romanticism is also imbued with the spirit of French Classicism, just as Claude's anticipations of Romanticism lead on naturally to Turner, Berlioz's contemporary.

Ex.3

It was in the nineteenth century that music and painting drew much closer together, when the Romantic impulse brought about a unity of feeling among artists of all kinds. In the visual arts, Romanticism found its fullest response in landscape, as painters like Friedrich and Turner celebrated the numinous quality in nature that poets such as Wordsworth and Hölderlin had proclaimed. In music, the overriding importance of form that had characterised the Classical style gave way to a new emphasis on content and individual feeling, and music too began to celebrate nature in a new and direct way.

A key work in the transition from Classicism to Romanticism is Beethoven's *Pastoral* Symphony, whose five movements have evocative titles: 'By the Brook', 'Peasants' Merry-making', 'Storm', and so on. Although Beethoven said that his music was "more feeling than painting", there is a certain amount of the latter: the storm is graphically portrayed, the motion of the brook is suggested by a constant undulation in the strings, and at the end of this movement the voices of nightingale, quail and cuckoo are imitated by flute, oboe and clarinet (Beethoven cleverly realising that two clarinets in unison convey the peculiarly muffled resonance of the cuckoo's call better than one). The *Pastoral* Symphony greatly influenced the early Romantics: the '*Scène aux champs*' in the *Symphonie fantastique* was Berlioz's direct response. Wagner's 'Forest Murmurs' from *Siegfried* are closely modelled on Beethoven's scene by the brook, with the same string undulations which become a background for bird-calls on the woodwind; though Wagner's birds make no attempt to imitate real sounds. Wagner employs musical metaphor rather than depiction, to make Berlioz's useful distinction, and the effect is more

Caspar David Friedrich: *Bohemian Landscape*, 1810

Gemäldegalerie, Dresden

Claude Lorraine: *Landscape with Ascanius shooting the stag of Sylvia*

Ashmolean Museum, Oxford

genuinely poetic.

Can we say more precisely why this should be so? In the *Ring*, as in his other mature works, Wagner used a complex musical language to express a multitude of feelings and ideas. In order to evoke nature, he chose an elemental means of expression: music based on the harmony of the triad. Since the Renaissance, the third has been considered the most consonant interval, and two superimposed thirds make up the triad, the basic chord of tonal music. Triadic harmony effectively symbolizes nature's simplicity and wholeness, in contrast with the complex, divided emotions of the gods and humans who upset the harmonious balance of nature that we are presented with at the start of the *Ring*. The moments of return to this original harmonious state — as in the 'Forest Murmurs' — are especially poignant, and Wagner is able to make these sonic landscapes as vividly real to the imagination as landscape paintings.

We should note that Wagner's stylized birdsong in the 'Forest Murmurs' is also based for the most part on the notes of the triad. Wagner's wisdom in avoiding over-literal imitation of natural sounds has not always been heeded. We might question whether Messiaen's progression from the magically potent birdsongs of the 'Liturgie de cristal' from *Quatuor pour la fin du temps*, which are not attempts at precise imitation and are simply marked 'comme un oiseau', to his scrupulously notated aviary of named species from all around the world in his later music is also an artistic advance. Listening to a piece like *Oiseaux exotiques*, I sometimes feel it is the product of an obsession that has got out of hand, and return gratefully to the calmer sound-world of the 'Liturgie de cristal', which is as exquisite an evocation of the dawn chorus as the famous one in Ravel's *Daphnis and Chloe*. Realism reaches its nadir in Respighi's *Pines of Rome*, in which he introduces a recording of a real nightingale: the effect is embarrassingly sentimental.

The limits of good taste and of artistic effectiveness are difficult to set, though it is easy enough to point to the episode with the bleating sheep in Strauss's *Don Quixote* as another lapse into the banality of literalism in what is otherwise a masterpiece. Strauss only too easily fell victim to his talent for imitating natural sounds. In the storm in his *Alpine Symphony*, Strauss uses wind and thunder machines for added realism, yet his torrents of sound fail to surpass the elemental power of Beethoven's storm in the *Pastoral* Symphony, which Beethoven achieves simply with timpani and the addition of two trombones to his modest orchestra, plus a piccolo for the lightning. 'Sound effects' percussion usually only works well in a humorous context, like Satie's typewriters in *Parade*. The wind machine can perhaps be justified in Vaughan Williams's *Sinfonia Antarctica* as a symbol of the inhumanity of nature in the icy wastes, though in his previous symphony Vaughan Williams had achieved a still more powerful effect of mysterious alienation through purely instrumental means. In Tippett's Fourth Symphony the composer at first used a wind machine to suggest the sounds of breathing that symbolize the beginning and end of life at the start and finish of this *Heldenleben*-like work. Finding this sound unsatisfactory, Tippett substituted a recording of actual breathing, with predictably ludicrous results: he has finally opted for a synthesized breathing sound. In fact all these artificial sounds are obtrusive, and it would have been better to use even so simple a device as overlapping cymbal rolls instead.

Throughout the nineteenth century, instrumental colour evolved as the orchestra gradually developed into the sophisticated and precise machine it had become by 1900. In the purest form of Classicism, the notes are all-important and their colouring irrelevant: thus in the *Art of Fugue*, Bach does not even specify which instruments the work is conceived for. A Beethoven symphony contains much orchestral colour, but can still be almost as effective when played on the piano. But already in Weber and Berlioz much of the effect is lost when the notes are transferred to the piano, while Schoenberg's Five Pieces for Orchestra or Sibelius's *Oceanides* or in fact almost any twentieth-century orchestral work cannot properly be appreciated without hearing the precise colour of the instruments for which it was written, in the same way that we can get little out of a black and white illustration of a late painting by Monet.

In *The Decline of the West,* Spengler makes eloquent and elaborate analogies between painting and music; in particular he finds a spiritual unity between the rise and triumph of oil painting from Giorgione to Rembrandt, and what he calls the pictorial music of that period, from Monteverdi to Lully and Purcell. There are indeed parallels to be drawn between composers and painters of the late Renaissance and Baroque: the romantic poetry of Giorgione finds an equivalent in the rich and strange melancholy of Gesualdo's madrigals, while the pageantry of Veronese's religious paintings could illustrate Monteverdi's *Vespers.* But in terms of technique, there is nothing in this music to match the sumptuous and subtle colours of Titian and Tintoretto, or the free brush-strokes in late Titian and Rembrandt that anticipate Turner and the Impressionists.

Although Monteverdi had a richly-coloured orchestra at his disposal for his operas (the orchestra for *Orfeo,* for instance, included 4 trumpets, 4 trombones, 2 cornetts, sopranino recorder, 3 archlutes, 2 chamber organs, regal, 2 harpsichords and strings), he did not orchestrate in the modern sense, but used homogeneous blocks of sound in a way perhaps analogous to fresco technique. In his revision of Berlioz's *Treatise on Instrumentation,* Richard Strauss draws attention to the different style of Wagner's orchestration to that of the Classical composers and compares it to the difference between the fourteenth and fifteenth-century Florentine painters and what he calls "the broad manner of Velasquez, Rembrandt, Franz Hals and Turner with their wonderfully shaded colour combinations and differentiated light effects". The specific example of Wagner's orchestration that Strauss uses to illustrate its differentiated colouring, the 'Magic Fire Music' from *Die Walküre* (Ex. 4), might find its visual equivalent in one of Turner's paintings especially concerned with capturing the brilliance of light. Turner and Wagner are rightly brought together as the two greatest nineteenth-century masters of colour in their respective arts. Strauss points particularly to the elaborate violin figurations in the 'Magic Fire Music': the four interweaving violin parts are overlaid with piccolos and harps, with added highlights on the glockenspiel. In a similar way Turner, in many of his sunrises, highlights his shimmering blend of colours with dabs of pure white to produce the effect of dazzling light.

Ex. 4

Wagner's successors continued to explore the orchestra's capacity to paint in sound -- or, perhaps more accurately, to find appropriate musical metaphors to evoke natural phenomena. The dominant orchestral form of the post-Wagnerian era was the symphonic poem, with its built-in programmatic element, a form that had been invented and first popularized by Liszt. Many symphonic poems were concerned in whole or part with metaphors from landscape: Wagner's 'Forest Murmurs' eventually found their apotheosis in Sibelius's *Tapiola*, that supreme evocation of the vast northern forests, whose mysterious, sometimes sinister power is finally revealed to have the capacity to console and heal -- an essentially Wagnerian concept. A number of symphonic poems were based on paintings. I know of two inspired by Böcklin's once-popular painting *The Isle of the Dead*, a dull one by Reger and the powerfully imaginative one by Rachmaninov, whose morbid temperament responded readily to the brooding, menacing intensity of Böcklin's vision.

Wagner's enormous influence pervaded all the arts from the 1860s until the beginning of the twentieth century. His doctrine of the *Gesamtkunstwerk*, the all-embracing work in which the various

J. M. W. Turner: *The Slave Ship*

Henry Lillie Pierce Fund
Courtesy, Museum of Fine Arts, Boston

Arnold Böcklin: *The Isle of the Dead*

Metropolitan Museum, New York

individual arts would be combined, assumed nonetheless that music would be supreme; and the supremacy of music was acknowledged in Pater's famous proclamation that all art aspires towards its condition (though Pater also stressed that each art has its own special and untranslatable quality of beauty).   This aspiration towards music may be variously observed in Whistler calling his paintings 'Nocturne' or 'Symphony'; in the symbolic paintings of Redon and Moreau; or even in Huysmans' novel *A rebours* about the ultimate aesthete, with his orchestra of liqueurs: "kümmel like the oboe with its sonorous, nasal timbre...gin and whisky raising the roof of the mouth with the blare of their cornets and trombones".

This is an eccentric form of synaesthesia -- the transference of the attributes of one sense to another.   A more common sort is the association of colour with sound.   Many composers have associated colours with particular keys: Beethoven spoke of B minor as black; E.T.A. Hoffmann described one of his characters as "the little man in a coat the colour of C sharp minor with an E major coloured collar"(!?).   Rimsky-Korsakov assigned to each key its specific colour: D major was yellow, E major blue, F major green, E flat major dark, gloomy blueish grey, and so on.   For what it's worth, I see D major as red and E flat as green, so the associations would seem to be entirely subjective, though I would guess that there might be some measure of agreement that sharp keys -- for example D or E -- are bright and flat keys more sombre, as all Rimsky-Korsakov's associations confirm.

In 1895, the artist and Professor of Fine Arts at Queen's College, London, Wallace Rimington, demonstrated his colour organ, a large box with a light inside and a number of apertures filled with coloured glass, which were opened and closed by a mechanism activated by a keyboard. Rimington accompanied performances of music, including orchestral music by Wagner, with projections of colour on to a screen.   In his colour organ, the seven diatonic notes of the scale, ascending from C, corresponded with the seven colours of the spectrum in ascending order from red (as suggested originally by Newton), with the chromatic notes combinations of the two adjacent colours. This correspondence was widely agreed on by turn-of-the-century occultists -- Madame Blavatsky and her circle; so it is not surprising that the Russian composer Scriabin, with his great interest in Theosophy and occultism in general, also made an attempt to combine colour and music. Scriabin was associated for a time with the Symbolist painters of the 'Blue Rose' group. He was influenced by Wagner, though somewhat wary of him, and his experience of hearing Wagner was limited -- he never heard *Tristan*, for instance. But Scriabin took Wagner's idea of the *Gesamtkunstwerk* beyond the Master's wildest fantasies. He planned the ultimate work of art, to be called *Mysterium*, in which music, words, dance, colour and scent would all be combined. It was to be performed in a temple in India and Scriabin, who was not a modest man, believed that it would literally bring about the end of the world. He died, however, at the age of 43, before he had done more than make preliminary sketches -- which was perhaps just as well for the world.

In his last completed orchestral work, *Prometheus, the Poem of Fire*, composed in 1910, Scriabin had included a part for a colour organ. His friend Alexander Mozer had made a similar instrument to Rimington's which was used at one of Scriabin's piano recitals, but the first performance of *Prometheus* in Moscow was given without any accompanying light effects. Colour projection was used at a performance in New York in 1915, just before Scriabin's death, but had no enlightening effect on the critics. No doubt the light projection was quite primitive, and so far as I know no attempt has yet been made to present the work as Scriabin envisioned, with the hall flooded with strong light rather than colours being projected on to a screen.

Scriabin used a different colour system to Rimington. He apparently recognized only three natural associations: C major was red, D major yellow and F sharp major blue. He derived the other colours by associating the spectral order with a rising progression of fifths, starting with C, red, and proceeding through G, orange; D, yellow; A, green; E, light blue...to F, dark red and back to C. C major for Scriabin symbolized matter and F sharp major spirit, and the central

part of *Prometheus* ascends from C to F sharp through a gradual
crescendo of harmony and colour. The colours correspond to the
fundamental progressions of the harmony: thus the light in theory
strengthens the sense of tonality by its synaesthetic relation. The
colour organ part is normally of two notes, or two colours, though
sometimes there is just a single colour and at just one point, three:
violet, dark red and green. At the opening of the piece, the long-held
chord, which Scriabin called his 'mystic chord', and the three-note
motif on horns, the basic motif of the piece and one which had
tremendous significance for Scriabin since it reappears in all his
subsequent music, are accompanied by a colour chord of blue and
green (Ex.5). Since this opening represents the dawn of creation, it
has been suggested that the colours may allude to the origin of life
in the sea, though Scriabin was not prone to such literalness. The
opaque luminosity of this opening chord is achieved by doubling
string tremolandi with low flutes, low clarinets and bassoons.
Prometheus ends in F sharp major, in a blaze of blue light, with
chorus and full organ joining the huge orchestra.

Ex.5

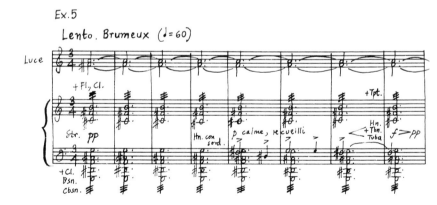

I must admit here that Scriabin's experiment with colour is
something of a red herring, though an irresistible one. It is best seen
as a precursor of experiments in the cinema, most famously Walt

Disney's *Fantasia*, and of the light shows that accompany present-day rock concerts. Let me return to my theme proper via a companion piece to *Prometheus* whose conception is even more cinematic, and which is the most achieved example of the *Gesamtkunstwerk*, Schoenberg's Expressionist opera *Die glückliche Hand*. Schoenberg wrote the text, 85% of which consists of stage directions, and designed costumes and scenery. At one point there are detailed directions for what Schoenberg calls a 'light crescendo', which closely parallel sections of *Prometheus*: "It begins with dull red light (from above) that turns to brown and a dirty green. Next it changes to a dark blue-grey, followed by violet. This grows in turn, into an intense dark red which becomes ever brighter and more glaring until after reaching a blood-red, it is mixed more and more with orange and then bright yellow; finally a glaring yellow light alone remains and inundates the second grotto from all sides."

The period of the composition of *Die glückliche Hand*, from 1910 to 1913, was also the climax of Schoenberg's activity as a painter. He had begun to paint around 1905, at about the time that he met the young painter Richard Gerstl, who painted a fine portrait of him in that year. Gerstl was passionately interested in music and an admirer of Schoenberg; Schoenberg in turn took painting lessons from Gerstl. Their friendship ended when in 1908 Gerstl persuaded Schoenberg's wife Mathilde to leave her husband for him; when Schoenberg persuaded Mathilde to return to him, Gerstl committed suicide. Though I don't want to labour the point, the fact that Schoenberg made his crucial breakthrough into Expressionism and to a musical language that abandoned tonality at the same time as this personal crisis is obviously no coincidence: to put it simplistically, Schoenberg found a heightened language to express what he was feeling. At the same time as he was writing his first non-tonal works —the song cycle *The Book of the Hanging Gardens*, the Five Orchestral Pieces and the two operas *Erwartung* and *Die glückliche Hand*, he was also painting intensively -- mostly portrait heads: many self-portraits and Expressionist heads which he called 'gazes'.

Schoenberg took his painting very seriously at this time. In an

Arnold Schoenberg: *The Source of Light* — sketch for Scene 2 of *Die glückliche Hand*

Arnold Schoenberg Institute, Los Angeles

Arnold Schoenberg: *Red Gaze*

Städtische Galerie im Lenbachhaus, Munich

interview he gave in 1949, the year before he died, he said: "It was the same to me as making music. To me it was a way of expressing myself, of presenting emotions, ideas, and other feelings." But whereas behind Schoenberg's Expressionist music is a masterly technique, the same cannot be said of Schoenberg's painting. Paintings such as *Red Gaze* come perilously close to the sort of art whose only virtue is its sincerity, and Schoenberg's arch rival Stravinsky would have been only too ready to remind him that "sincerity is a *sine qua non* that at the same time guarantees nothing." In 1910, Schoenberg exhibited 40 of his paintings at a gallery in Vienna: they were received with as much hostility as his recent music. But Schoenberg found a champion in Kandinsky, with whom he had begun to correspond in 1911, and who included Schoenberg's paintings in the first *Blaue Reiter* exhibition at the end of that year, along with Marc, Delaunay and Henri Rousseau.

Schoenberg's first letter to Kandinsky is a fulsome response to the older artist sending him a portfolio of his work. Schoenberg agrees that the two of them have much in common, and that both of them are concerned with the direct expression of intuitive feelings. Kandinsky's development from Symbolism to abstraction, which closely parallels Schoenberg's development towards musical Expressionism, was conceived by him in terms of an attempt to make his paintings produce more and more the effect of music. The strongly contrasting colours that he began to use around 1908 he believed would make his paintings sing out more resonantly and produce strong, pulsating rhythms. In 1909, the year that Schoenberg finally forsook tonality, Kandinsky was still painting landscapes, but the next logical stage was to abandon representation in favour of a purely abstract play of colours, the interrelations of which would, he hoped, produce a more precise equivalent to a musical composition with its elements of melody, harmony and counterpoint. In these first abstract paintings, Kandinsky, like Scriabin (with whom he shared an interest in Theosophy), used a spectral scale, with each colour assigned a definite meaning. Kandinsky wrote extensively about the language of colour in his book *Concern-*

ing the Spiritual in Art, both in general terms -- yellow is "the typically earthly colour"; blue "the typically heavenly colour", green "the most restful colour that exists" -- and also by making particular analogies with musical instruments: "Light blue is like a flute, a darker blue a cello; a still darker a thunderous double bass; and the darkest blue of all -- an organ", and so on.

We may make of these analogies what we choose. I know that when I look at Kandinsky's abstract paintings I don't 'hear' the instruments Kandinsky was hearing. The language for me is purely visual and I have no need to relate it to music. In fact the particular associations that Kandinsky makes are a distraction; an interesting distraction, but a distraction none the less. They were means to an end, which was to give the paintings their resonance and depth. In his book *Theoria*, Peter Fuller wrote of the relation of Kandinsky's work to icon painting, and this seems to me a more immediately meaningful connection. Kandinsky was a religious man, who remained loyal to the Orthodox faith in which he was brought up, and his ultimate aim was that his paintings should communicate a spiritual experience, which I think the best of them do. Scriabin was attempting the same in his music. Kandinsky was more successful, as Scriabin's egotism and the overwhelming aroma of hedonistic sexuality keep obscuring the intended spirituality. There are times, however, when I find myself agreeing with what Ernest Newman said about *Prometheus*, that "the wind that blows through the music is the veritable wind of the cosmos itself".

The relationship between abstract painting and music is best explored, I think, from the painter's point of view. As a composer I don't find that abstract painting is necessarily closer to music than representational painting, especially since I'm not happy to speak of music as an abstract language. Schopenhauer, who seems to me to have been the most perceptive of philosophers who have written about music, was right when he said that "Music...if regarded as an expression of the world, is in the highest degree a universal language...Its universality, however, is by no means that empty universality of abstraction, but quite of a different kind, and is united

Wassily Kandinsky: *Autumn Study*, 1910

Städtische Galerie im Lenbachhaus, Munich

Wassily Kandinsky: *Composition IV*, 1911

Kunstsammlung Nordrhein-Westfalen, Düsseldorf

Piet Mondrian: *Composition with Red, Yellow and Blue*, 1927

Stedelijk Museum, Amsterdam

with thorough and distinct definiteness." Mendelssohn confirmed
this when he said that what music expresses is "not too indefinite to
be put into words, but on the contrary too definite". The kind of
definiteness that music has may best be seen in painting that is at the
same time representational and symbolic --its most proper function,
as has been apparent since the invention of photography took over
from painting its purely representational mode. It is here that music
and painting may sometimes share common ground, as when I
compared Friedrich and Bruckner who had each found a precise
means within their own art of symbolizing their similar experience
of the world.

Having said this, I do think that certain parallels may be drawn
between abstract painting and the development of non-tonal music
since Schoenberg, and particular correspondences between particular artists. For example, Webern and Mondrian, both of whom
began with a firm grounding in tradition, and who gradually worked
through to a radical language whose rigorous purity eliminated
everything but essentials. Both of them also had a strongly religious
sensibility. The counterpoint of single notes in Webern's later
work, in particular a piece such as the middle movement of the
String Quartet, op.28 (Ex.6), where the structure is audibly sym-
metrical, is matched by Mondrian's structured counterpoint of
colour in his late paintings. Though I should point out that
Mondrian himself might not have agreed with this analogy, for we
know that in calling his last paintings 'Boogie Woogies' he then at
least had in mind quite another musical correspondence.

Ex. 6

The weight of meaning that we sense behind each one of Mondrian's squares of colour, or each of Webern's notes, could not, however, be passed on automatically to their successors. Webern along the way to his mature style had sacrificed so much of what hitherto had been thought essential in a piece of music -- melody and harmony in their traditional sense -- that those composers who chose to take Webern as their starting point were in potential danger of producing no more than contrasting patterns of sound. I have no space here to go further into that particular problem; but I want at least to mention Peter Fuller's long preoccupation with the equivalent situation in painting, where he saw in late Modernist abstraction what he called a *kenosis*, or emptying out of value, so that unlike Kandinsky or Mondrian, or indeed Rothko, colours are nothing but colours. I shall return later to the solutions he was beginning to propose to what he saw was a spiritual crisis in art. But I must go back to Schoenberg where I left him.

While Kandinsky was trying to paint music, Schoenberg, in one piece he wrote in the summer of 1909, the third of his Five Pieces for Orchestra, op.16, tried to compose a landscape -- or rather the impression of sunlight on the water of the Traunsee, a lake in Upper Austria, as he had seen it once at dawn. He translated his impressions into a series of quiet, overlapping chords, scored with extreme subtlety for a large orchestra. Ex.7 shows the opening of the piece. The prevailing stillness is occasionally disturbed: at one point by what Schoenberg said was a jumping fish, and we may hear others; while in the middle there is a sudden shift of colours -- perhaps a cloud passing over the sun, or a brief shower -- before the original calm is restored. Despite this literalness to his subject, Schoenberg was initially reluctant to disclose the source of his inspiration, eventually agreeing to call the piece 'Farben' ('Colours') when his publisher asked him for a title. A diary entry made at this time reveals a somewhat tortuous anxiety not to give anything away, which may largely be put down to the constant ridicule that he was used to receiving from hostile critics. Though since the piece came wholly out of his imagination and was not based on someone else's

The Traunsee, Upper Austria

J.M.W. Turner: *Waves Breaking Against the Wind*

Tate Gallery, London

idea of a lake, he may well have wished simply to trust his audience's
intuition, for he retained the confident belief that those who under-
stood his music would understand *everything* he said in it.

Ex.7

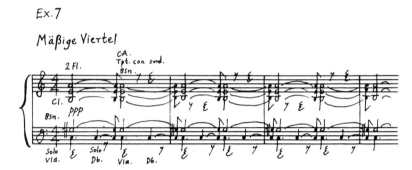

I want to compare 'Farben' with two other evocations of dawn
over water, in both cases the sea rather than a lake: the opening of
Debussy's *La mer* (Ex.8), and the 'Dawn' Interlude from Britten's
Peter Grimes (Ex.9). In both these pieces there is, I think, a more
immediate visual element than in the Schoenberg piece. Schoenberg,
as an Expressionist, is as much concerned, or more, with what he
feels as what he sees, and even in 'Farben' it is hard to get away from
Schoenberg's intensely introspective feelings about what he is
looking at, which seem curiously to drain the light away from the
colours. Schoenberg would probably have agreed that he was not
attempting to achieve the kind of objective vision one senses more
strongly in the Debussy and the Britten, one more obviously
detached from the feelings that engendered it. Debussy's attitude
here is of course similar to the Impressionists with whom he has
often been compared.

Each of these three composers has tried to express the idea of calm
by the obvious means of prolonged, quiet sounds. But Schoenberg
is concerned with absolute stillness, and the gradual colour changes
that come about through almost imperceptible shifts of light. So his
piece is, harmonically, almost entirely static. In *La mer* we straightaway

sense movement: there is a rapid tracing of a line from the soft
timpani roll in the bass with which the piece begins to the high violin
tremolo, like a sweep from shore to horizon or from sea to sky. This
high and low unison on the note B leaves a great space in between,
which the woodwind fill with a phrase, already anticipated by the
cellos, that suggests a perceptible swell of waves. This may be a
calm sea, but there's always a feeling of restlessness.

Ex. 8

Ex. 9

Britten, who would have known *La mer* well and not wanted to
reduplicate its opening, begins at the opposite extreme of the
orchestra with a high, unaccompanied violin line, for the sky, and

brings the ear down through the clarinet and viola flourishes to the soft brass chords -- the great expanse of the sea itself. What movement there is in Britten's sea picture is contained within the progression of these brass chords away from and then back to their initial A major; we sense the latent menacing power of the sea, which later in the opera will explode into a violent storm.

The sea has been a major source of inspiration for British composers since the renaissance of British music at the end of the nineteenth century. The Romantic quest for divinity in nature found a place, in this country especially, for the spirits of meadows, groves and streams; though most of its yearning was directed towards the infinite rather than the intimate. The most appropriate symbols of infinity in nature are mountains, forests and the sea, and for the British the sea is the most potent of these. There are thousands of British seascape paintings, though not many that go beyond the simply pictorial. Turner's are pre-eminent: such paintings as his *Yacht Approaching the Coast* in the Tate Gallery, or another wonderful late study of a rough sea, *Waves Breaking Against the Wind*, the very essence of sea-ness. Other painters who have captured something of the sea's essence include Steer, with several paintings of the sea at Walberswick -- the *Peter Grimes* sea -- and Lowry, whose late studies of the sea have a bleak but compelling poetry.

Confronted with the sea as a subject, composers' and painters' attitudes are sometimes very similar. In Eric Fenby's memoir of Delius there is a famous account of the blind, paralysed composer dictating to Fenby the opening of his orchestral piece *A Song of Summer*. Delius approaches his task just like any *plein air* painter setting up his canvas: "I want you to imagine", he tells Fenby, "that we are sitting on the cliffs in the heather overlooking the sea. The sustained chords in the high strings suggest the clear sky, and the stillness and calmness of the scene." To this he adds a phrase in the cellos and basses "to suggest the gentle rise and fall of the waves", and a figure on solo flute which "suggests a seagull gliding by". The image of the blind composer trying to express directly what he sees in his mind is a poignant one, even if the actual result here, as with

all the music that Fenby nobly took down, pales in comparison with
what Delius had written in the vigour of his earlier life. The
ingredients themselves are not at fault -- sea, sky and the frail
presence of a living creature: what else is there in a sea picture? The
same kind of opening recurs in other English musical seascapes --
in Bax's *Tintagel*, or Frank Bridge's *The Sea*, which was the first
orchestral piece that Britten heard, as a boy; as he said later, he was
"knocked sideways" by it. The opening of *The Sea* might almost be
a realisation of Delius's description, with Bridge's oboe taking the
place of Delius's flute. This splendid music succinctly illustrates
the special flavour of English musical Romanticism: the high level
of emotion coupled with an appealing earnestness.

I want to go back now to Britten's *Peter Grimes* sea and look at
it in more detail. It's a less overtly Romantic evocation than Bridge's,
but even more typically English in the way powerful emotions are
suggested but are always held in check. I would claim that it is just
this quality of restraint that gives the music its special strength,
because Britten is able to objectify his emotions into something akin
to Classicism. This objectivity is apparent in the musical material
Britten uses to create his sea picture. There are three ideas, as I have
already mentioned. The first is the high melodic line for violins that
represents the sky. If it were just violins, the purity of their tone
might have suggested an unclouded blue; but the stage directions
indicate "a cold grey morning", so Britten doubles the violins with
two flutes, which dull the violins' bright overtones and help evoke
one of those high, wide, leaden skies typical of the east coast -- this
is the sea at Aldeburgh where *Peter Grimes* is set and where Britten
lived. We might go further in pictorial analogy and suggest, as some
commentators have done, that the wheeling movement of this
melodic line portrays gulls wheeling in the sky; and indeed a herring
gull's call might well be stylized into the appoggiatura F-E that we
constantly hear. We can relate this slow wheeling to the faster
wheeling movement of the second idea, the flourishes for clarinets
and violas, which again might suggest seabirds, or could relate to
waves breaking on the shore; and if we take them as that, then they

could form a link to the third idea, the brass chords that represent the
sea. But there is no need at all to impose literal description on this
material, and Britten deliberately keeps it at the level of metaphor
rather than depiction. In fact we might consider the three ideas in
a purely formal way, noting how Britten places them, introducing
them separately and though later allowing them to overlap, never
obscuring their separateness: they are like three distinct subjects or
areas of colour in a painting.

Though separate and distinct, all three ideas are unified by their
grounding in the interval of the third which, as Christopher Palmer
has pointed out, symbolized a state of nature for Britten as it had
done for Wagner. It was Britten more than any other composer who
restored potency to the triad at a time when others were pronouncing
it, and the tonal system that was founded on it, dead. The soft brass
triads here, deep and dense, have a similar natural authority to the
triadic leitmotifs of the *Ring*, or the brass chorale at the end of the
first and third movements of *La mer* -- to which they are most
obviously related. The clarinet and viola flourishes are built out of
a chain of thirds, the same notes that, strung out in a line, form the
high violin melody.

Lastly the orchestration: I mentioned the deliberate dulling of the
violins' melodic line; the orchestral colours overall are sombre, but
always clear, never hazily impressionistic. The flourishes for clarinets doubling violas are also outlined by the harp and so made to
stand out strongly against their background. Even the brass chords
are subdued in colour, especially because the trumpets are kept in
what Palmer calls "their lowest plain-chocolate-brown or black-
grey register". Palmer quotes Percy Grainger's observation that an
instrumentation of "mainly neutral tints" is appropriate to the
depiction of nature at her sublimest and at the same time most
monotonous, as the desert or the sea, to support his argument, with
which I agree, that the monotonal colouring of the 'Dawn' Interlude
enhances its elemental power. We might say the same of the
monotonal horns at the start of *Das Rheingold* -- another evocation
of watery nature -- or remember the veiled opening of *Prometheus*,

possible another underwater picture.

I have considered Britten's 'Dawn' Interlude in some detail because it seems to me a particularly striking example of a composer responding to Ruskin's advice to the painter, to "go to Nature in all singleness of heart...having no other thoughts but how best to penetrate her meaning". And though I have concentrated on the sea as an image of nature, I am aware that the English landscape has provided a still richer stimulus for composers, as it has, of course, for English painters. If I'd had space, I could have chosen many pieces by Elgar, Delius, Vaughan Williams, Holst or Tippett, whose visionary strength derives from a similarly deep response to nature in the English landscape. The opening of Vaughan Williams's Fifth Symphony (Ex.10) might be *the* archetypal English landscape in sound. Precisely why this should be so is difficult to say: we can talk loosely of its roundness, its soft edges; we can point out that the scale on which the music is based is one most characteristic of English folk music -- the major scale with flattened seventh. Clearly Vaughan Williams's understanding of English musical tradition and his love of his native landscape came together, at this particular moment during the Second World War when everything he most cherished was under threat of destruction, to produce this especially resonant sound-image.

Ex.10

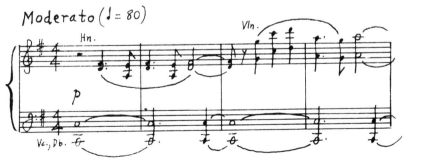

I could also have shown how the tradition of response to nature has continued in British music of the present day. Peter Maxwell Davies for instance has chosen to live in the wildest and remotest possible landscape, the island of Hoy in Orkney, in order to let its spirit suffuse his music. Of his Second Symphony he has written that is "not only a direct response to the sounds of the ocean's extreme proximity, subtly permeating all of one's existence...but also a more considered response to the architecture of its forms." And we may feel in the rough, gritty grandeur of some of Harrison Birtwistle's music an equally direct response to landscape, and particularly to the stark Pennine landscape in which he was brought up.

Landscape, then, has been as important a factor in the renaissance of British music since Elgar as it has been in British painting, but what had begun in painting in the first flowering of Romanticism, with Cotman and Constable, did not begin in British music until a century later, by which time there was a whole tradition of Romantic response to nature to take on board, which had almost reached a point of exhaustion on the continent of Europe. In Britain, Elgar, by sheer force of genius, created a fresh tradition, which his successors inherited (even if some of them may have thought they were reacting against it). But can we still "go to Nature in all singleness of heart"? If we are bent on making this world a wasteland, how can we continue to derive creative nourishment from nature? I only raise that huge question because to ignore it altogether would be to live in invincible ignorance; but I can't begin to try to answer it adequately here. I can only say that, for myself, I still feel strongly linked to that English tradition I have mentioned, and that in trying to write music I have been aware of the frailty of nature, but also of her continuing sustaining power, which perhaps, to paraphrase Hopkins, deep down is never spent. Peter Fuller showed how the struggle to redeem a wounded landscape had been a source of strength for painters such as Spencer, Paul Nash or Sutherland. In their case it was a landscape scarred by war; but the image of the wounded landscape, precariously poised between frail beauty and destruction, persists, and the alternative to continuing the struggle

Cecil Collins: *The Music of Dawn*

Courtesy Anthony d'Offay Gallery, London.

to redeem it is, Peter felt, to lapse into futility. I feel a heartening sense of kinship when I look at the work of those painters whom Peter singled out as having achieved a redemptive vision of contemporary landscape. I am thinking especially of Australian painters such as Russell Drysdale, Fred Williams, Sydney Nolan and Arthur Boyd, as well as others in this country — Ivon Hitchens, Frank Auerbach, William Tillyer. Such artists Peter saw as upholding the values of traditional sensibility in opposition to the vacuity and spiritual deadness of much of what he saw elsewhere in the contemporary art world (a vacuity I should say that doesn't exist to nearly the same extent in the world of serious music, at least, perhaps for the simple reason that there is no money to be made out of it).

I want to end with an English painter who became more and more important to Peter in the last years of his life, as an emblematic figure of the values he was defending, and who has also become very important to me: Cecil Collins. Collins's last major painting was *The Music of Dawn.* By an uncanny coincidence Peter talked about this painting in the last lecture he gave, a few days before his death, and at the same time I was writing an orchestral piece based on the painting, which I had seen in the Collins retrospective at the Tate Gallery in 1989, a few days after Collins's own death. Collins was one of the most musical of painters, and in giving this painting such a title he was almost inviting a musical response to it. He was already able to express in painting so much of what music, in its distillation of the essence of things, attempts also to reach.

Although Collins was thoroughly modern in his awareness of the world around him, he was only too sure about rejecting what he saw as false in modern life, as when in his essay *The Vision of the Fool* he quotes from Jacques Maritain: "the modern world is shaping human activity in a properly inhuman way...for the ultimate end of all this frenzy is to prevent man from remembering God." Peter used to keep on insisting that he was an atheist, while recognizing the paradox that the redemptive vision is extraordinarily difficult unless it is allied to some kind of religious view of the world. It looks as if, when Peter died, he was moving towards such a religious view, but who can tell where his journey might have ended? Collins himself, though no orthodox believer, had the clearest perception of what he knew to be eternally true. In a painting such as *The Music of Dawn*, there is not only a fraternal relation with medieval and early Renaissance art -- with Fra Angelico's angel choirs -- but also with the unclouded vision of the early Romantics, with Blake and Palmer. Landscape and symbolism come together here with wonderful purity and freshness: the sea, the new sun, the image of the divine in the guise of a woman. "Through the forms and symbols of the angelic", Peter wrote, "Collins takes us beyond subsuming vacuity...beyond the terrible inertia of matter." Painters and composers alike must continue to engage with this terrible inertia, and hope to transcend it.